SMILE and SCALE

With

By

George Knowlton

Dedication

This book is dedicated to the visionaries and value-driven leaders who believe that business can be both profitable and principled.

To every entrepreneur who wants to grow without burning out, to every business owner seeking alignment between wealth and wellness, and to every innovator exploring how AI can elevate—not replace—human potential: this is for you.

Let this book serve as your roadmap to an ethical, scalable, AI-powered future. Whether you're starting from scratch or fine-tuning a thriving company, may these pages equip you with clarity, confidence, and the courage to lead with heart and data.

Together, we're not just building businesses—we're building legacies.

Acknowledgement

First and foremost, thank you, God, for the vision, grace, and resilience to bring this book into being. Your guidance through every twist and triumph continues to shape my purpose and passion.

To my family—thank you for being my grounding force. Your unwavering love, encouragement, and belief in me provided the emotional runway for this journey. You gave me the confidence to dream boldly, and the safe space to build something greater than myself.

To my friends—thank you for the long talks, the late-night strategy sessions, and the much-needed humor when the work felt heavy. Your presence in my life is a source of joy, perspective, and inspiration.

To my colleagues, collaborators, and the brilliant minds behind SMILE Company and TIDE 360—you are the engine behind this movement. Your commitment to ethical innovation, sustainable growth, and financial empowerment has been the heartbeat of every word written. Each insight you contributed, every project we built together, shaped the essence of this book.

And to the early readers, the curious thinkers, and the action-takers who continue to explore new frontiers with us—thank you for trusting this message. You are the reason we scale with purpose and lead with integrity.

Table of Contents

Introduction: The Future of AI and Business Success 1

Why AI is the Ultimate Game-Changer for Entrepreneurs 1

The SMILE Philosophy for Ethical, Sustainable Innovation 2

The Wealthy & Healthy Mindset for Business Growth 3

What You'll Learn in This Book 4

Are You Ready to Scale with AI? 5

Why TIDE 360? Because Innovation Should Be Simple & Sustainable 5

Chapter 1: The AI Revolution – Why Now is the Time to Innovate 7

Introduction: The Business World is Changing—Are You Ready? .. 7

The AI Boom: Why This Moment is Different 8

The Biggest Opportunities AI Creates for Business Owners 9

The Cost of Hesitation: What Happens If You Ignore AI? 12

How Businesses Are Already Using AI to Scale and Win 12

The Time to Leverage AI is Now 13

How TIDE 360 Keeps You Ahead of the Curve 14

Why Most AI Strategies Fail (And How TIDE 360 Fixes This) 15

Why TIDE 360 is the Best Solution for AI Innovation 16

Are You Ready to Lead the AI Revolution? 17

Chapter 2: The SMILE Framework for AI-Powered Business Growth 18

Introduction: Why You Need a System for AI Success 18

The Five Pillars of the SMILE Framework 19

How to Apply the SMILE Framework to Your AI Strategy 22

How to Implement SMILE with TIDE 360 23

Final Thoughts: SMILE as the Key to Sustainable AI Growth 23

Chapter 3: AI-Powered Automation – Work Less, Earn More 25

Introduction: The Secret to Scaling Without Burnout 25

The Truth About AI Automation: It's Not About Replacing You—It's About Freeing You 26

The 5 Areas of Business That AI Can Automate Today................. 27

How to Automate Your Business with AI in 5 Simple Steps 29

Final Thoughts: Automation is the Key to Time & Financial Freedom 31

How to Start Automating with TIDE 360 in 5 Steps 32

Chapter 4: The Wealthy & Healthy Approach to AI Strategy............ 33

Introduction: AI Should Build Wealth, Not Just Cut Costs 33

AI as an Investment, Not an Expense 34

Sustainable Growth: Balancing Automation and Human Talent 35

Case Studies: Businesses Thriving with AI-Powered Innovation... 36

How to Apply the Wealthy & Healthy AI Strategy to Your Business 37

Final Thoughts: AI is Your Growth Engine—Use it Wisely........... 39

Chapter 5 AI-Driven Marketing – Personalization & Profitability at Scale.. 40

How AI is Transforming Digital Marketing 40

How to Implement AI in Your Marketing Strategy..................... 43

Final Thoughts: AI Marketing is the Future—Are You Ready? 45

Chapter 6: AI-Powered Finance – Smarter Money Management....... 46

Introduction: Why AI is the Future of Financial Management....... 46

Why AI is Revolutionizing Finance................................ 47

5 Ways AI is Transforming Financial Management.................. 48

How to Implement AI in Your Business Finances 50

Final Thoughts: AI Makes Money Management Smarter & Easier 52

Chapter 7 AI and Leadership – How to Build a Future-Proof Business 53

Introduction: The Future of Leadership is AI-Driven.................. 53

Why AI is the Secret Weapon for Modern Leaders 54

The 5 Ways AI is Transforming Leadership 55

How to Integrate AI into Your Leadership Strategy 58

Final Thoughts: AI Leadership is the Future – Will You Adapt?.... 59

Chapter 8 The Future of AI & Business Innovation – What's Next? . 60

Introduction: AI is Just Getting Started 60

The 5 Biggest AI Trends That Will Shape the Future of Business . 61

How Businesses Must Prepare for the Future of AI 64

Final Thoughts: AI is the Future—Are You Ready?.................... 66

Chapter 9: Your AI Business Action Plan – Implement AI the Right Way with TIDE 360 67

Introduction: AI is the Future—TIDE 360 is the Solution 67

Your AI Business Roadmap with TIDE 360 68

Why Businesses Trust TIDE 360 for AI Integration 71

Final Thoughts: AI is the Future—TIDE 360 is the Solution 72

Introduction to the Journaling Section 73

Chapter 1: The AI Revolution – Why Now is the Time to Innovate
.... 76

Chapter 2: The SMILE Framework for AI-Powered Business Growth
.... 81

Chapter 3: AI-Powered Automation – Work Less, Earn More 86

Chapter 4: The Wealthy & Healthy Approach to AI Strategy 91

Chapter 5: AI-Driven Marketing – Personalization & Profitability at
Scale 96

Chapter 6: AI-Powered Finance – Smarter Money Management . 101

Chapter 7: AI and Leadership – How to Build a Future-Proof
Business 106

Chapter 8: The Future of AI & Business Innovation – What's Next?
.... 111

Chapter 9: Your AI Business Action Plan – Implement AI the Right
Way with TIDE 360 116

Introduction:
The Future of AI and Business Success

Why AI is the Ultimate Game-Changer for Entrepreneurs

Imagine having a business that runs smoothly, makes data-driven decisions, and generates revenue 24/7—without you constantly managing every detail. **What if you could work fewer hours while increasing profits, improving customer experiences, and making smarter, faster decisions?** This is no longer a futuristic dream—it's what AI makes possible today.

Artificial intelligence (AI) is **reshaping how businesses operate**, helping entrepreneurs and business owners **automate repetitive tasks, optimize decision-making, and personalize customer interactions at scale.** It's **not about replacing people—it's about creating a wealthier, healthier, and more innovative way to run a business.**

Businesses that embrace AI now will **thrive**. Those that hesitate risk getting left behind. **The question is not IF you should integrate AI into your business, but HOW you will leverage it for success.**

The SMILE Philosophy for Ethical, Sustainable Innovation

With any major technological shift, there's a right way and a wrong way to innovate. That's where the **SMILE framework** comes in. This approach ensures that AI is used ethically, strategically, and sustainably, balancing profitability with integrity.

The **SMILE framework** consists of five pillars:

- **Safety** – AI should be used to **enhance security, efficiency, and stability**, not create chaos or risk job losses.
- **Morality** – AI should align with ethical values, ensuring **fairness, inclusivity, and responsible automation.**
- **Inclusivity** – AI should **expand opportunities** for all—customers, employees, and entrepreneurs alike.
- **Linguistic Clarity** – AI should be **easily understood**, helping businesses communicate clearly with their audiences.
- **Experiential Learning** – AI should **improve real-world experiences**, both for businesses and their customers.

By following this framework, businesses can harness AI to scale without sacrificing ethics, customer trust, or human engagement.

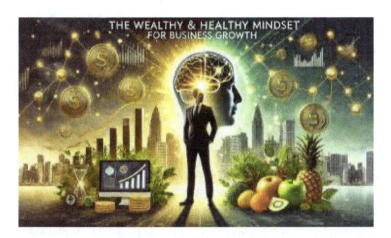

The Wealthy & Healthy Mindset for Business Growth

AI isn't just a tool—it's a **strategy for creating wealth and sustainability.** But to fully benefit from it, entrepreneurs must adopt the **right mindset.**

A wealthy & healthy business mindset means:

- **Working smarter, not harder** – Automating repetitive tasks so you can focus on high-value activities.

- **Building long-term success** – Using AI to grow a **scalable** business that doesn't require constant oversight.

- **Balancing automation with human touch** – Keeping **human creativity, leadership, and emotional intelligence** at the core of business operations.

- **Staying ahead of the curve** – Understanding that the world is moving toward **AI-driven decision-making**, and businesses that leverage it now will dominate in the future.

This book will show you **how to integrate AI into your business effectively**—whether you're a solo entrepreneur, a small business owner, or a CEO scaling a company. You'll learn how to **automate processes, maximize efficiency, increase revenue, and future-proof your business—all while maintaining ethical and sustainable growth.**

What You'll Learn in This Book

This book is your step-by-step guide to **leveraging AI for maximum business growth and innovation.** Throughout these chapters, you'll discover:

- **How AI is transforming industries** and why now is the time to adopt it.
- **The SMILE framework for AI-powered success,** ensuring ethical and effective integration.
- **AI automation strategies** that save time, reduce costs, and boost productivity.
- **The best AI tools** for marketing, finance, customer service, and leadership.
- **How to use AI-driven analytics** to make smarter business decisions.
- **How AI can help you build a scalable, profitable business** while reducing burnout.

Are You Ready to Scale with AI?

By the time you finish this book, you'll have a **clear roadmap** to implementing AI in a way that's profitable, sustainable, and ethical. **The AI revolution is here. The question is: Will you be a leader or a spectator?**

Why TIDE 360? Because Innovation Should Be Simple & Sustainable

AI is **the most powerful business tool of our time**, but too many companies approach it incorrectly. Instead of **enhancing business operations**, they:

- **Waste money on AI tools they don't understand**
- **Overcomplicate the process and frustrate their teams**
- **Automate without strategy, leading to costly mistakes**

At **TIDE 360**, we do things differently.

We created the **SMILE system** to ensure AI integration is:

- **Strategic** – AI should work with your current processes, not against them.
- **Measurable** – AI should have **clear financial benefits** and ROI.
- **Inclusive** – AI should **enhance human potential**, not replace it.
- **Long-term** – AI should be **scalable, flexible, and future-proof**.
- **Ethical** – AI should be used responsibly, aligning with your values.

When you follow the **TIDE 360 roadmap**, AI becomes:

- **A tool for acceleration, not confusion.**
- **A bridge to greater wealth and efficiency.**
- **A strategic asset that sets you apart from competitors.**

By the end of this book, you'll have **a clear plan to integrate AI into your business using TIDE 360's proven methods.**

Let's dive in!

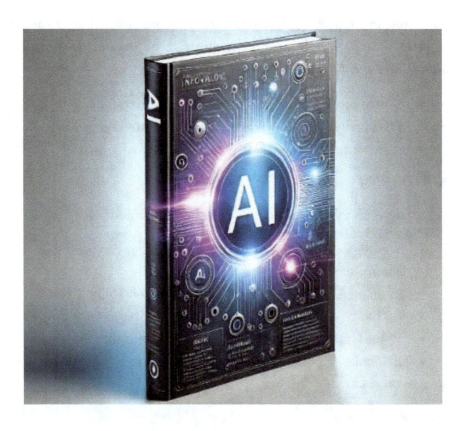

Chapter 1:
The AI Revolution – Why Now is the Time to Innovate

Introduction: The Business World is Changing—Are You Ready?

AI is no longer a futuristic concept—it's here, and it's reshaping **every industry** at an unprecedented pace. Whether you run a small business, a growing startup, or a multi-million-dollar enterprise, **AI is transforming how work gets done, how customers interact with brands, and how businesses scale faster than ever before.**

The question isn't whether AI will impact your business—it's whether you'll **leverage it to your advantage** or struggle to keep up while competitors automate, optimize, and dominate.

This chapter explores:

- **Why AI adoption is accelerating faster than ever**
- **The biggest opportunities AI creates for business owners**
- **The real risks of ignoring AI—and how to avoid falling behind**
- **How businesses are already using AI to increase profits and efficiency**

By the end of this chapter, you'll see why **the businesses that embrace AI now will be the market leaders of tomorrow.**

The AI Boom: Why This Moment is Different

AI has been around for years, but 2025 marks a **tipping point**—one where AI has become more powerful, more affordable, and easier to integrate into everyday business operations.

Here's why AI adoption is exploding right now:

1. AI is More Accessible Than Ever

- You don't need a massive budget or a team of engineers to integrate AI into your business.
- AI tools are now **affordable, easy to use, and customizable** for businesses of all sizes.
- Platforms like ChatGPT, Jasper AI, and MidJourney allow **small businesses to automate content, marketing, and customer support.**

2. AI is Driving Unprecedented Business Growth

- Businesses that integrate AI see an **average revenue increase of 20-40%** in the first year.
- AI-powered **chatbots, automation, and analytics** are helping businesses scale while reducing costs.
- AI is allowing businesses to **expand without hiring massive teams—creating efficiency and profitability.**

3. AI is No Longer Optional—It's Necessary for Survival

- Businesses that ignore AI will fall behind competitors who **automate faster, personalize customer experiences, and make smarter decisions with AI-driven data.**

- AI isn't just improving business processes—it's **changing customer expectations** and industry standards.
- **Customers now expect AI-driven personalization, instant support, and predictive recommendations.**

If you **hesitate** to integrate AI, your competitors will **adopt, automate, and dominate**—and you'll be left playing catch-up.

The Biggest Opportunities AI Creates for Business Owners

AI isn't just about replacing tasks—it's about unlocking **new opportunities** that **weren't possible before.** Here's how AI is transforming business across different areas:

1. AI Automates Repetitive Work—So You Can Focus on Growth

- AI-powered assistants handle **emails, scheduling, customer support, and data entry** automatically.
- Chatbots can **answer FAQs, qualify leads, and assist customers 24/7** without human involvement.
- AI can **write blog posts, generate reports, and create marketing content** in seconds.

Example: A solopreneur using AI for scheduling, marketing, and lead follow-ups can **double productivity without hiring extra staff.**

2. AI Creates Ultra-Personalized Customer Experiences

- AI analyzes customer behavior and **tailors product recommendations, email campaigns, and advertisements** for each user.
- AI-powered chatbots offer **instant, data-driven customer support** without long wait times.
- AI tracks user data to predict customer needs—allowing businesses to **sell smarter and build deeper relationships.**

Example: Netflix and Amazon use AI to **recommend movies and products before customers even know they want them.** Your business can do the same.

3. AI Improves Decision-Making and Business Strategy

- AI crunches **millions of data points** in seconds—giving business owners **real-time insights** into sales, trends, and customer behavior.
- AI-powered analytics help businesses **predict market trends, optimize pricing, and make better financial decisions.**
- AI can even **forecast demand**—helping businesses prepare for busy seasons or slow periods.

Example: AI-powered data tools can tell you which products will sell best next quarter—helping you make smarter inventory and marketing decisions.

4. AI Enhances Marketing and Sales Like Never Before

- AI can generate **high-converting ad copy, emails, and social media content** in minutes.
- AI chatbots and automation tools can **qualify leads, book appointments, and close deals 24/7.**
- AI-driven **A/B testing** helps businesses optimize sales pages and advertising campaigns **automatically.**

Example: AI tools like Jasper AI and Copy.ai are already helping businesses **write ad copy, product descriptions, and social media content that drives sales.**

5. AI Cuts Costs While Increasing Efficiency

- AI-powered automation allows businesses to **do more with fewer employees—reducing overhead.**
- AI can **detect fraud, prevent errors, and improve cybersecurity**—saving businesses from costly mistakes.
- AI reduces waste and inefficiency—**maximizing productivity and profitability.**

Example: A business using AI-powered accounting software can **automate bookkeeping, track expenses, and detect financial risks**—without hiring a full-time accountant.

The Cost of Hesitation: What Happens If You Ignore AI?

Many business owners hesitate to adopt AI because they:

- Fear AI is "too complicated" or expensive
- Worry about losing the "human touch" in their business
- Don't fully understand how AI can help them

But waiting **too long** to integrate AI comes with **real risks**:

- **You'll Fall Behind Competitors** – Businesses using AI will **scale faster, sell smarter, and automate operations—leaving others behind.**
- **You'll Lose Customers to AI-Optimized Businesses** – AI-powered businesses **deliver faster, more personalized, and more efficient customer experiences.**
- **You'll Waste Time and Money on Manual Work** – While others **cut costs and boost profits**, AI-hesitant businesses will **struggle to keep up.**

The truth is: Businesses that hesitate to embrace AI today will be playing catch-up tomorrow.

How Businesses Are Already Using AI to Scale and Win

- **eCommerce**: AI-powered recommendation engines increase sales by **up to 30%** by suggesting the right products at the right time.
- **Marketing**: AI-driven tools create high-converting ads, emails, and landing pages in **minutes, not hours.**
- **Finance**: AI-powered bookkeeping software saves businesses **thousands** by **detecting fraud and automating accounting.**

- **Customer Service**: AI chatbots handle **80% of customer inquiries automatically**—reducing support costs and response times.

Businesses in every industry are leveraging AI to increase revenue, reduce costs, and improve efficiency.

The Time to Leverage AI is Now

AI is the **most powerful business tool of our time**—and it's only getting smarter, faster, and more essential.

This isn't just about keeping up—it's about **gaining an edge**. If you integrate AI into your business **today**, you'll have a **competitive advantage for years to come**.

In the next chapter, we'll break down **the SMILE Framework**—a proven system for integrating AI **ethically, efficiently, and profitably** into your business.

Are you ready to build a business that runs smarter, faster, and more profitably?

Let's move forward.

How TIDE 360 Keeps You Ahead of the Curve

The Business Landscape is Changing—Are You Ready?

Artificial Intelligence is not coming—it's already here. The question isn't **if** AI will impact your business, but **how soon** and **how prepared you are for it**.

- **AI-driven companies are scaling 5x faster than traditional businesses.**
- **AI-powered automation is eliminating inefficiencies in every industry.**
- **AI is becoming a core part of decision-making, customer engagement, and operations.**

However, most businesses struggle with AI adoption because they:

- **Don't know where to start**
- **Fear AI will replace human creativity and jobs**
- **Waste money on AI tools without a strategy**

This is why **TIDE 360 exists**—to **remove the guesswork and complexity from AI adoption**.

Why Most AI Strategies Fail (And How TIDE 360 Fixes This)

Many businesses jump into AI **without a roadmap**, leading to:

- **Wasted money on unnecessary AI tools**
- **Confusion and resistance from employees**
- **Lack of clear results or ROI**

At **TIDE 360,** we use a structured, phased approach that ensures **seamless AI adoption** without overwhelm.

- **Phase 1: AI Discovery & Strategy** – Identify **how AI fits into your business**
- **Phase 2: SMILE Framework Implementation** – Create **a sustainable AI roadmap**
- **Phase 3: AI Scaling & Automation** – Optimize **operations, sales, and customer engagement**

Instead of buying random AI tools and hoping for the best, we custom-build AI solutions designed to maximize efficiency, profitability, and scalability.

Why TIDE 360 is the Best Solution for AI Innovation

TIDE 360's AI Services: Your Competitive Advantage

TIDE 360 provides **AI-powered solutions at every level** of business, ensuring you stay ahead of the curve:

TIDE 360 Webinar (The Starting Point)

- Learn how AI is revolutionizing business in 2025 and beyond
- Discover how AI-driven businesses scale faster with fewer resources
- Get a free SMILE system eBook ($27 Value)

TIDE 360 Agents ($297/month – AI Support On Demand)

- **AI Virtual Assistants** – Automate scheduling, emails, and admin tasks
- **AI Financial Analysts** – Optimize bookkeeping, invoicing, and cost management
- **AI Marketing Agents** – Automate social media, content, and advertising

TIDE 360 Coaching & Consulting (For Deeper AI Integration)

- **6-Week AI Group Coaching ($997/person)** – Learn AI adoption strategies step-by-step
- **12-Week AI Implementation Coaching ($9,997)** – Hands-on AI business transformation
- **Done-for-You AI Business Automation (Starting at $49,997)** – Full AI integration tailored to your needs

No wasted time. No confusion. Just a proven AI system designed to scale your business.

Are You Ready to Lead the AI Revolution?

AI isn't coming—it's here. And businesses that embrace **TIDE 360's AI-powered solutions** now will:

- **Outperform competitors**
- **Scale faster with fewer resources**
- **Future-proof their operations for long-term success**

In the next chapter, we'll break down **TIDE 360's SMILE Framework**—your step-by-step guide to sustainable AI integration.

Let's dive in!

Chapter 2:
The SMILE Framework for AI-Powered Business Growth

Introduction: Why You Need a System for AI Success

AI is the most powerful business tool of our time—but **without a system, AI can create more confusion than clarity**. Many businesses rush to integrate AI without a clear strategy, leading to wasted resources, ethical concerns, and frustrated teams.

The **SMILE Framework** provides a structured, ethical, and effective way to **integrate AI into your business without the chaos**. This system ensures that AI is **profitable, sustainable, and aligned with your core values**—helping you scale while maintaining trust with your customers and employees.

No more guesswork. No more AI overwhelm. Just clear, strategic growth.

This chapter explores:

- **The five pillars of the SMILE Framework and why they matter**
- **How to apply these principles to your AI-powered business strategy**
- **Real-world examples of businesses using SMILE to scale successfully**

By the end of this chapter, you'll know exactly how to implement AI in a way that maximizes profits while keeping your business ethical, inclusive, and future-proof.

The Five Pillars of the SMILE Framework

Safety: Implementing AI Without Risking Security or Jobs

AI should be a **tool for empowerment—not a threat** to job security, privacy, or stability. Many businesses fail to consider the risks of AI, such as:

- **Data privacy violations** – Mishandling AI-generated customer data can lead to legal trouble and loss of trust.
- **Job displacement** – Replacing human workers too quickly can damage morale and hurt brand reputation.
- **AI bias & misinformation** – Poorly trained AI can make **unethical decisions**, leading to discrimination or incorrect data.

How to Implement AI Safely in Your Business

- **Use AI to support, not replace, your team** – Automate repetitive tasks so employees can focus on high-value work.
- **Ensure data security & compliance** – Work with AI tools that protect customer information and follow regulations.
- **Monitor AI decisions for accuracy** – Regularly audit AI-generated insights to prevent misinformation and bias.

Example: A company using AI-powered hiring software discovered that the system unintentionally favored certain demographics. By **auditing and retraining the AI**, they ensured fair hiring practices and avoided potential lawsuits.

Morality: Ethical AI Integration for Sustainable Business Practices

AI should align with **ethical values and long-term sustainability**, not just short-term profit. Businesses that cut corners with AI often face **customer backlash, legal trouble, or reputation damage**.

How to Use AI Ethically in Your Business

- **Be transparent with your customers** – Let users know when they're interacting with AI vs. a human.
- **Avoid AI shortcuts that exploit customers** – Don't use AI to manipulate or mislead buyers.
- **Choose AI partners wisely** – Work with companies committed to responsible AI development.

Example: In 2024, a well-known eCommerce brand used AI to **auto-generate fake product reviews**—causing a major scandal. The backlash led to lost customers and legal consequences. **Honesty and transparency always win.**

Inclusivity: Leveraging AI to Expand Your Customer Reach

AI should open doors for more people, not exclude them. Many businesses unknowingly use AI that alienates customers due to bias, poor accessibility, or lack of cultural awareness.

How to Use AI to Promote Inclusivity

- **Test AI-generated content for bias** – Ensure AI-powered ads, chatbots, and hiring software work fairly for all demographics.
- **Make AI-powered tools accessible** – Use AI-driven voice assistants, screen readers, and translations to **serve a diverse audience**.
- **Train AI to recognize global markets** – Optimize AI for different languages, cultural nuances, and user behaviors.

Example: A streaming platform used AI to **recommend content based on diverse user backgrounds**, boosting engagement by **40%**. By

making AI more inclusive, they expanded their reach and built a stronger global audience.

Linguistic Clarity: Communicating AI Benefits Effectively to Your Audience

AI is only useful if **people understand it**. Many businesses make the mistake of using **overcomplicated AI jargon**, confusing both employees and customers.

How to Improve AI Communication in Your Business

- **Avoid technical jargon in AI-powered services** – Use simple, clear language when explaining how AI tools work.
- **Educate customers on AI's role** – Show them how AI helps improve their experience **without replacing human support**.
- **Train employees on AI integration** – Make sure your team understands **how to use AI effectively** instead of fearing it.

Example: A bank introduced AI-powered customer support but **didn't explain how it worked**. Customers got frustrated when AI chatbots couldn't handle complex requests. Once the bank **reworded their chatbot scripts and added an option to talk to humans**, satisfaction rates increased by **55%**.

Experiential Learning: Using AI to Improve Customer & Employee Experience

AI should enhance **real-world experiences**, not just automate processes. The best businesses use AI to **make life easier, faster, and more enjoyable** for their teams and customers.

How to Improve AI-Powered Experiences

- **Personalize AI recommendations** – Use AI to suggest products, services, or solutions tailored to each customer.
- **Use AI to enhance—not replace—human interactions** – Blend automation with **personalized customer service** for a seamless experience.
- **Keep AI adaptive & evolving** – Regularly update AI tools based on customer feedback and employee insights.

Example: An online clothing store used AI to offer personalized size recommendations, reducing returns by 30%. AI didn't just speed up the process—it improved the entire shopping experience.

How to Apply the SMILE Framework to Your AI Strategy

Now that you understand the **five pillars of SMILE**, here's how to **apply them** when integrating AI into your business:

- **Step 1: Identify Areas for AI Integration** – Look at your **most time-consuming, repetitive tasks** and see where AI can help.
- **Step 2: Choose Ethical AI Tools** – Research AI tools that prioritize **security, inclusivity, and user experience**.
- **Step 3: Start Small & Test** – Implement AI in **one area at a time**, measure results, and adjust as needed.

- **Step 4: Train Your Team** – Ensure employees understand **how AI helps them rather than replaces them**.
- **Step 5: Regularly Evaluate AI Performance** – Keep checking AI accuracy, customer feedback, and security updates.

This **SMILE-powered AI strategy** will help any business integrate AI effectively, ethically, and profitably.

How to Implement SMILE with TIDE 360

- **Step 1: Assess your current AI readiness** (TIDE 360 AI Audit)
- **Step 2: Develop a customized AI roadmap** (SMILE Strategy Session)
- **Step 3: Implement AI step-by-step** (TIDE 360 Agents & Automation)
- **Step 4: Measure AI impact and optimize** (TIDE 360 Growth Dashboard)

AI should **simplify, not complicate** your business. **TIDE 360** ensures AI is implemented the **right way**—so you see measurable results fast.

Final Thoughts: SMILE as the Key to Sustainable AI Growth

AI is a **powerful tool for scaling your business**, but only if used responsibly and strategically. The **SMILE Framework** helps you:

- **Integrate AI without losing human connection**
- **Avoid ethical and security pitfalls**
- **Ensure AI serves customers of all backgrounds**
- **Keep AI simple and understandable for employees & customers**

- **Use AI to create better experiences, not just faster automation**

The businesses that embrace AI with strategy, ethics, and clarity will dominate in the future economy.

Chapter 3:
AI-Powered Automation – Work Less, Earn More

Introduction: The Secret to Scaling Without Burnout

What if your business could run smoothly, generate revenue, and handle customer interactions—all while you focused on the bigger picture?

- **Imagine cutting your workload in half while doubling your productivity.**
- **Imagine a business that operates 24/7—even when you're sleeping or on vacation.**
- **Imagine automating the tasks that drain your time, so you can focus on what truly matters.**

This isn't a fantasy—it's what AI-powered automation makes possible.

In this chapter, you'll discover how to:

- Use AI to automate repetitive tasks, saving hours every day
- Increase revenue while reducing costs through AI-driven efficiency
- Avoid common automation mistakes that lead to frustration instead of freedom
- Find the right AI tools for your business and integrate them seamlessly

By the end of this chapter, you'll have a **clear roadmap** to implementing AI-powered automation in a way that makes your business more profitable, efficient, and stress-free.

The Truth About AI Automation: It's Not About Replacing You—It's About Freeing You

One of the biggest fears business owners have about AI is **"Will it replace me or my team?"**

The answer is no—AI is not here to take over. It's here to handle the repetitive, time-consuming tasks that keep you from focusing on growth and strategy.

- AI doesn't replace leaders—it empowers them.
- AI doesn't kill jobs—it eliminates the boring, repetitive parts of jobs.
- AI doesn't remove the human touch—it enhances it by letting you focus on high-value work.

Automation isn't about doing less—it's about doing more of what actually matters.

The 5 Areas of Business That AI Can Automate Today

AI automation can **boost productivity, reduce errors, and increase profits** by optimizing the most time-consuming tasks in your business. Here's where AI delivers the biggest impact:

1. AI-Powered Marketing Automation

- **Email Marketing** – AI can write, schedule, and optimize email campaigns for better open rates.
- **Ad Campaigns** – AI-powered ad platforms adjust bids, target the right audience, and improve conversion rates automatically.
- **Social Media Posting** – AI tools like Buffer and Hootsuite schedule and optimize content posting across platforms.
- **Content Creation** – AI can generate blog posts, video scripts, and social media captions in seconds.

Example: A small business using AI-powered email automation increased **customer engagement by 45%** while reducing manual work by **60%**.

2. AI-Driven Customer Service & Sales

- **AI Chatbots** – AI-powered assistants handle FAQs, process orders, and provide instant support 24/7.
- **Automated Lead Qualification** – AI can identify hot leads, saving sales teams from wasting time on unqualified prospects.
- **AI-Powered Voice Assistants** – AI phone systems can book appointments, answer inquiries, and manage customer interactions.

Example: A company that replaced human-only customer service with **AI-assisted chatbots** reduced response times by **80%** and **cut costs by 50%** while maintaining excellent customer satisfaction.

3. AI for Financial & Business Operations

- **AI Accounting & Bookkeeping** – AI tools like QuickBooks automate invoicing, expense tracking, and fraud detection.
- **AI-Powered Pricing Strategies** – AI analyzes competitors' pricing and market trends to adjust prices in real time.
- **Payroll & HR Automation** – AI-powered HR tools can onboard employees, track performance, and automate payroll.

Example: A business using AI-driven pricing adjustments increased sales by **30%** by offering the **right prices at the right time** without manual effort.

4. AI for Productivity & Task Management

- **Automated Scheduling** – AI assistants like Calendly handle meeting bookings without back-and-forth emails.
- **AI-Powered Virtual Assistants** – AI assistants handle reminders, transcribe meetings, and even draft emails.
- **Task Prioritization** – AI analyzes workflows and suggests **which tasks are most urgent and important.**

Example: A startup using AI-powered scheduling tools saved **15+ hours per week** by eliminating manual calendar management.

5. AI-Powered Personalization & Customer Experience

- **Smart Product Recommendations** – AI predicts what customers will buy next based on behavior and data.
- **AI-Powered Personal Shopping Assistants** – AI helps customers find products faster through voice search and chatbots.
- **Automated Customer Feedback Analysis** – AI scans reviews and customer feedback to detect trends and areas for improvement.

Example: An eCommerce business using AI-generated personalized product recommendations **boosted sales by 40%** without increasing marketing spend.

How to Automate Your Business with AI in 5 Simple Steps

Now that you know **where AI can help,** let's talk about **how to implement automation the right way**—without overwhelming your team or customers.

Step 1: Identify Your Biggest Time Drains

Ask yourself:

- **What tasks do you and your team do repeatedly?**
- **What slows down your workflow?**
- **What could be done faster or more efficiently with automation?**

Example: If your team spends **10+ hours a week answering the same customer inquiries**, AI-powered chatbots can save time while improving response speed.

Step 2: Choose the Right AI Tools

Not all AI tools are created equal. Look for:

- **Ease of use** – Can your team adopt it quickly?
- **Customization** – Can it adapt to your business needs?
- **Integration** – Does it work with your existing systems?

Recommended AI Tools:

- **Marketing Automation:** HubSpot, Jasper AI, Copy.ai
- **Customer Service:** ChatGPT-powered chatbots, Drift, Zendesk AI
- **Finance & Accounting:** QuickBooks AI, Xero, Bill.com
- **Productivity & Scheduling:** Calendly, Motion AI, Notion AI

Step 3: Test and Adjust in Small Steps

- **Start with ONE** automation at a time to see how it works.
- **Monitor performance** and adjust settings based on feedback.
- **Keep an option for human intervention** where needed.

Example: A company implementing AI-powered email marketing tested **5 different subject lines** using AI recommendations. The AI-optimized email had **a 60% higher open rate.**

Step 4: Train Your Team on AI-Powered Workflows

- **Teach employees how AI works** and how it helps—not replaces—them.
- **Encourage employees to embrace AI** by showing them how it makes their jobs easier.
- **Create AI-human collaboration strategies** where automation supports—but doesn't eliminate—human roles.

Example: A sales team using AI lead scoring **reduced wasted time by 50%**, allowing reps to **focus on high-value leads** instead of chasing low-probability prospects.

Step 5: Scale Up & Optimize for Maximum Results

- **Once an AI system works well,** expand its role in other areas of your business.
- **Regularly analyze automation performance** and adjust AI settings based on results.
- **Stay ahead of AI trends** to keep improving efficiency and profitability.

Example: An online business that started with **AI-powered customer support** later expanded to AI-driven sales forecasting, marketing automation, and pricing adjustments—doubling revenue in one year.

Final Thoughts: Automation is the Key to Time & Financial Freedom

- **AI-powered automation is not about working less—it's about working smarter.**
- **AI allows businesses to scale without burnout, reduce costs, and increase profitability.**
- **The companies that automate NOW will lead their industries in the years ahead.**

In the next chapter, we'll dive into **AI in marketing—how to use AI to attract, convert, and retain more customers while spending less on advertising.**

Ready to make AI marketing work for you? Let's go!

How to Start Automating with TIDE 360 in 5 Steps

- **Step 1:** Identify the biggest time-wasting tasks in your business.
- **Step 2:** Choose an AI automation tool that aligns with your needs (TIDE 360 Agents).
- **Step 3:** Implement AI in one area first (customer service, marketing, or finance).
- **Step 4:** Track improvements and optimize AI workflows.
- **Step 5:** Scale AI automation across multiple business functions.

TIDE 360 ensures **seamless AI automation**, helping you:

- **Save time, reduce costs, and increase efficiency.**
- **Focus on strategy while AI handles the day-to-day operations.**
- **Scale your business without overworking yourself.**

In the next chapter, we'll explore **how AI-driven marketing with TIDE 360 can increase leads and revenue effortlessly.**

Let's go!

Chapter 4:
The Wealthy & Healthy Approach to AI Strategy

Introduction: AI Should Build Wealth, Not Just Cut Costs

Many businesses look at AI as just another expense—a necessary cost to stay competitive. But the smartest companies don't see AI as an expense; they see it as an investment—one that generates massive returns when implemented correctly.

- **AI isn't about replacing people—it's about empowering them.**
- **AI should create long-term value, not short-term fixes.**
- **AI, when used strategically, leads to higher revenue, lower costs, and sustainable business growth.**

At **TIDE 360**, we believe AI should make your business both **WEALTHY** and **HEALTHY**—financially strong, efficient, and built to last.

In this chapter, you'll learn how to:

- **View AI as an investment that generates measurable ROI**
- **Balance AI automation with human talent for sustainable growth**
- **See real-world examples of businesses thriving with AI-powered innovation**

By the end of this chapter, you'll understand how to use AI to create a **scalable, profitable, and future-proof business.**

AI as an Investment, Not an Expense

Many businesses hesitate to invest in AI because they worry about upfront costs—but what they fail to realize is that **AI pays for itself**.

The True ROI of AI

Businesses that successfully integrate AI see:

- **25-50% cost savings** from automation and efficiency improvements
- **Higher employee productivity** as AI eliminates repetitive tasks
- **Faster decision-making** with AI-powered data analysis
- **Increased revenue** through AI-driven personalization and marketing

AI doesn't just save money—it makes money.

Example: American Express uses AI-driven fraud detection to **save billions**. By investing in machine learning, they have drastically reduced fraudulent transactions, protecting revenue while improving customer trust.

Best AI ROI Tracking Tools:

- Google Analytics AI
- IBM Watson Analytics
- Tableau AI

Sustainable Growth: Balancing Automation and Human Talent

A common fear with AI is that it will replace human workers—but the truth is, AI is most powerful when it **enhances human capabilities**.

- **AI automates repetitive tasks so employees can focus on high-value work.**
- **AI makes jobs easier, not obsolete—freeing up time for innovation and creativity.**
- **AI + Human Expertise = The Ultimate Competitive Advantage.**

The "Wealthy & Healthy" AI Balance

The best AI strategies focus on three key areas:

1. **Automate What's Repetitive** – AI should handle data entry, scheduling, and customer inquiries so people can focus on growth.
2. **Empower Employees with AI Tools** – AI should support human talent, not replace it (e.g., AI-driven analytics for better decision-making).
3. **Maintain the Human Touch** – Use AI for efficiency, but ensure customer relationships and creativity remain human-led.

Example: Starbucks uses AI-powered sales forecasting to optimize inventory—but **baristas and customer service remain human-driven**, keeping the brand experience personal.

Best AI Workforce Optimization Tools:

- Asana AI
- Clockwise
- Receptivity AI

Case Studies: Businesses Thriving with AI-Powered Innovation

Case Study #1: AI-Powered Personalization – Netflix's Recommendation Engine

- **Challenge:** Netflix needed a way to keep users engaged and reduce subscription cancellations.
- **AI Solution:** They developed an AI-driven recommendation engine that predicts what users want to watch.
- **Results:** 80% of content watched on Netflix comes from AI-powered recommendations—leading to higher engagement and retention.
- **Takeaway:** AI-driven personalization boosts customer satisfaction and revenue.

Case Study #2: AI in Retail – Walmart's Smart Inventory Management

- **Challenge:** Walmart needed to prevent inventory shortages and overstocking.
- **AI Solution:** AI-driven analytics predict product demand based on location, season, and shopping trends.
- **Results:** Walmart cut inventory costs by billions while ensuring stores are stocked with the right products at the right time.
- **Takeaway:** AI-driven supply chain management saves money and improves efficiency.

Case Study #3: AI in Marketing – Coca-Cola's AI-Powered Ad Campaigns

- **Challenge:** Coca-Cola wanted to create more personalized, engaging marketing campaigns.
- **AI Solution:** AI analyzes consumer behavior and generates data-driven ad creatives.
- **Results:** AI-powered ads increased customer engagement and improved return on advertising spend (ROAS).
- **Takeaway:** AI-driven marketing improves audience targeting and campaign performance.

How to Apply the Wealthy & Healthy AI Strategy to Your Business

Step 1: Identify AI Opportunities That Improve ROI

- **Where is your business wasting time or resources?**
- **Which tasks could AI automate without sacrificing quality?**
- **Where could AI help increase sales, efficiency, or customer satisfaction?**

Example: If responding to customer emails takes too much time, an AI chatbot could handle FAQs instantly—**improving response time and customer experience**.

AI Opportunity Identification Tools: Zapier AI, Drift, IBM Watson AI

Step 2: Implement AI Where It Enhances, Not Replaces, Human Talent

- **Choose AI tools that support employees instead of replacing them.**
- **Use AI to handle repetitive, time-consuming tasks.**
- **Ensure employees are trained to work alongside AI.**

Example: AI-powered transcription tools like **Otter.ai** save time by automatically summarizing meetings—**allowing teams to focus on execution instead of note-taking**.

AI Workforce Support Tools: Notion AI, Grammarly AI, Clockwise

*****

Step 3: Track AI Performance & Optimize for Long-Term Growth

- **Measure AI's impact on revenue, productivity, and customer satisfaction.**
- **Regularly adjust AI strategies based on performance data.**
- **Continuously refine AI tools to maximize ROI.**

Example: AI-driven marketing automation led to a **30% increase in engagement** for one company—but after optimizing AI-driven ad targeting, engagement increased to **50%**.

Best AI Performance Tracking Tools: Google Analytics AI, HubSpot AI, Salesforce Einstein

Final Thoughts: AI is Your Growth Engine—Use it Wisely

- AI should make your business both WEALTHY (profitable) and HEALTHY (sustainable).
- AI is an investment, not an expense—when used strategically, it delivers exponential returns.
- Balancing AI with human talent creates a business that is both scalable and customer-focused.

Now is the time to start implementing AI the RIGHT way—ensuring long-term success without sacrificing the human touch.

In the next chapter, we'll dive into AI-powered marketing—how businesses are using AI to personalize customer experiences and increase revenue effortlessly.

Ready to make AI work for you? Let's go!

Chapter 5
AI-Driven Marketing – Personalization & Profitability at Scale

AI is Changing the Marketing Game—Are You Ready?

Marketing used to be about **guesswork**—businesses spent money on ads, hoping they would reach the right audience.

- **Today, AI eliminates guesswork by predicting exactly what customers want.**
- **AI allows businesses to create hyper-personalized experiences at scale.**
- **AI-powered automation ensures marketing campaigns run efficiently—24/7.**

Companies using AI-driven marketing strategies are seeing:

- **Higher engagement and conversions** – AI ensures the right message reaches the right person at the right time.
- **Reduced ad costs** – AI optimizes targeting, reducing wasted spend.
- **Stronger customer relationships** – AI-powered personalization makes marketing feel human.

In this chapter, we'll explore how real-world brands use AI to increase sales, improve engagement, and cut costs.

How AI is Transforming Digital Marketing

Here are five ways AI is making marketing smarter, more efficient, and more profitable.

1. AI-Powered Content Creation & Copywriting

- AI can generate blogs, ads, and email copy in seconds—saving businesses hours.
- AI tools like Jasper, Copy.ai, and ChatGPT create SEO-optimized articles that rank higher on Google.
- Marketers can produce content faster, while AI refines tone and style.

Real-World Example: Forbes uses AI-powered content creation tools to generate finance and sports articles. AI scans trends and writes data-driven reports instantly—allowing Forbes to publish breaking news faster than competitors.

AI Content Tools to Try:

Jasper AI,Copy.ai, ChatGPT

2. AI-Driven Email Marketing & Customer Engagement

- AI-powered emails personalize subject lines, content, and send times for better engagement.
- Automated email sequences guide customers through sales funnels without human effort.
- AI analyzes user behavior, ensuring email campaigns target the most engaged customers.

Real-World Example: Netflix uses AI to send personalized recommendations via email. Based on watch history and preferences, AI suggests new shows, increasing engagement and user retention.

AI Email Marketing Tools to Try:

Mailchimp AI, ActiveCampaign, Klaviyo

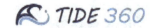

3. AI-Powered Social Media & Paid Advertising

- AI automates social media posting, ensuring brands stay active without manual effort.
- AI ad platforms analyze user behavior and optimize campaigns for better ROI.
- AI-driven A/B testing finds the best-performing ads instantly.

Real-World Example: Coca-Cola uses AI-powered social media analysis to detect trends and predict customer sentiment. This allows them to adjust ad campaigns in real-time—before engagement drops.

AI Social Media Tools to Try:

Hootsuite AI, Sprout Social, Adzooma

4. AI-Powered Chatbots & Customer Support

- AI chatbots handle customer inquiries 24/7—reducing wait times and improving experience.
- Chatbots can answer FAQs, process orders, and provide personalized product recommendations.
- **AI helps businesses handle customer service without needing massive support teams.**

Real-World Example: H&M uses an AI chatbot to provide fashion advice based on user preferences. Instead of waiting for a human stylist, customers get instant outfit recommendations—improving shopping experiences.

AI Chatbot Tools to Try:

Drift, Intercom, ManyChat

5. AI-Driven Predictive Analytics & Customer Insights

- AI predicts customer behavior, allowing businesses to tailor marketing strategies.
- AI identifies high-value customers—helping businesses focus efforts where they matter most.
- AI detects purchasing patterns, allowing for personalized offers and discounts.

Real-World Example: Amazon's AI-driven recommendation engine accounts for 35% of total sales. AI tracks purchase history and browsing behavior—suggesting products customers are most likely to buy next.

AI Predictive Analytics Tools to Try:

Google Analytics AI, HubSpot AI, Salesforce Einstein

How to Implement AI in Your Marketing Strategy

Step 1: Identify Areas Where AI Can Improve Marketing

- Which marketing tasks take too much time?
- Where do I struggle with engagement or conversions?
- Which areas of my marketing feel like guesswork?

Example: If email engagement is low, AI-powered personalization tools can increase open rates by 60% or more.

Step 2: Choose the Right AI Marketing Tools

- **AI for Content Creation:** Jasper, Copy.ai, ChatGPT
- **AI for Email Marketing:** ActiveCampaign, Klaviyo, Mailchimp AI
- **AI for Social Media & Ads:** Adzooma, Hootsuite AI, Canva Magic Write

- **AI for Customer Insights:** Google Analytics AI, Salesforce Einstein

Step 3: Test AI in One Area First

- Start small – Implement AI in one area first (e.g., email automation).
- Monitor results – Measure open rates, engagement, and conversions.
- Optimize & expand – Once AI is working well in one area, apply it to others.

Example: A business started by automating email follow-ups and later expanded AI into ad targeting, content creation, and chatbot automation.

Step 4: Monitor & Optimize AI Performance

- Regularly analyze AI-generated content & campaigns to ensure effectiveness.
- Combine AI with human creativity – AI helps scale marketing efforts, but human input keeps messaging authentic.
- Stay updated on AI trends – New AI marketing tools emerge constantly—early adopters gain a competitive edge.

Example: A business using AI-generated ads saw a 30% increase in conversions—but when combined with human storytelling, conversions jumped to 50%.

Final Thoughts: AI Marketing is the Future—Are You Ready?

- AI marketing is not just a trend—it's the new standard for businesses that want to grow faster, spend less, and engage customers at scale.
- AI helps businesses automate, personalize, and optimize marketing efforts effortlessly.
- The businesses that integrate AI now will dominate their industries in the next decade.

In the next chapter, we'll explore AI in finance—how AI is making money management smarter, safer, and more profitable.

Ready to make AI work for your business? Let's go!

Chapter 6:
AI-Powered Finance – Smarter Money Management

Introduction: Why AI is the Future of Financial Management

Money management has always been one of the biggest challenges for businesses. Tracking expenses, budgeting, forecasting, and preventing fraud require time and expertise. In the past, companies relied on spreadsheets, accountants, and manual calculations.

- Today, AI is transforming finance—making money management smarter, faster, and more accurate.
- AI-powered tools can track cash flow, predict financial trends, and detect fraud—all automatically.
- Businesses using AI-driven finance strategies are reducing costs, increasing profits, and making better financial decisions.

In this chapter, you'll learn how to:

- Use AI to automate bookkeeping, invoicing, and payroll
- Leverage AI for smarter budgeting, forecasting, and fraud detection
- Improve cash flow and increase profitability with AI-driven financial insights

By the end of this chapter, you'll know how to implement AI to take full control of your business finances—without stress or errors.

Why AI is Revolutionizing Finance

Traditional financial management is:

- **Time-consuming** – Manual bookkeeping and tracking require hours of work.
- **Error-prone** – Human mistakes in accounting can lead to major financial losses.
- **Reactive, not proactive** – Traditional methods focus on past data instead of predicting future financial trends.

But AI is here to assist:

- AI solves these problems by automating financial tasks and providing real-time insights.
- AI can analyze millions of data points instantly—helping businesses make better financial decisions.
- AI eliminates human errors in accounting, forecasting, and fraud detection.

Companies using AI-powered finance tools report:

- 30-50% savings in administrative costs
- More accurate cash flow predictions and budgeting
- A drastic reduction in fraud and financial risks

5 Ways AI is Transforming Financial Management

1. AI-Powered Bookkeeping & Accounting

- AI tools automate expense tracking, categorization, and report generation.
- AI-powered bookkeeping software reduces human errors in financial statements.
- AI can instantly generate profit and loss reports, tax documents, and balance sheets.

Real-World Example: Xero, an AI-powered accounting platform, reduces financial reporting time by 90%. Businesses using Xero automate tax preparation, invoice tracking, and payroll processing—eliminating manual errors.

AI Accounting Tools to Try: QuickBooks AI, Xero, FreshBooks

2. AI for Smart Budgeting & Cash Flow Forecasting

- AI predicts future revenue and expenses based on historical data and market trends.
- AI alerts businesses about potential cash flow shortages before they happen.
- AI provides automated suggestions for cost-cutting and budget optimization.

Real-World Example: Float, an AI-driven cash flow management tool, helped businesses reduce budget overruns by 25%. AI detects spending patterns and automatically adjusts budgets to prevent financial waste.

AI Budgeting & Forecasting Tools to Try: Float, Vena, Planful

3. AI-Powered Fraud Detection & Security

- AI scans financial transactions in real-time to detect fraudulent activity.
- AI prevents unauthorized access and flags suspicious transactions instantly.
- AI-based fraud detection reduces chargebacks, cybercrime, and identity theft.

Real-World Example: PayPal's AI fraud detection system analyzes millions of transactions per second. AI detects fraud 30% faster than traditional methods—saving businesses billions in losses.

AI Fraud Detection Tools to Try:

Kount, Riskified, Feedzai

4. AI for Automated Payroll & Invoicing

- AI ensures employees are paid on time by automating payroll processing.
- AI-generated invoices track payments and follow up on overdue accounts automatically.
- AI reduces errors in salary calculations, tax deductions, and employee benefits.

Real-World Example: ADP's AI-powered payroll system automates salary distribution for over 810,000 businesses. AI calculates taxes, benefits, and overtime pay without manual input.

AI Payroll & Invoicing Tools to Try:

Gusto, Paychex, Bill.com

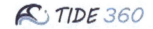

5. AI in Business Investments & Pricing Strategies

- AI analyzes stock market trends, helping businesses make smarter investment decisions.
- AI-powered pricing tools adjust product prices in real-time based on demand and competition.
- AI helps businesses forecast profitability before making big investments.

Real-World Example: Uber's AI-driven dynamic pricing model adjusts ride fares in real time based on demand. This pricing strategy increases revenue while ensuring competitive pricing for customers.

AI Investment & Pricing Tools to Try:

Kavout, Zacks AI, Pricefx

How to Implement AI in Your Business Finances

Step 1: Identify Your Financial Pain Points

- Which financial tasks take up too much time?
- Where are human errors affecting my financial reporting?
- Where could AI help improve cash flow and prevent fraud?

Example: If manual bookkeeping takes too long, AI-powered accounting software can automate data entry, categorize expenses, and generate reports instantly.

Step 2: Choose AI Tools That Fit Your Business

- **AI for Bookkeeping & Accounting:** QuickBooks AI, Xero, Zoho Books
- **AI for Budgeting & Forecasting:** Float, Planful, Vena
- **AI for Fraud Detection & Security:** Kount, Riskified, Forter
- **AI for Payroll & Invoicing:** Gusto, Paychex, Wave

- **AI for Investments & Pricing:** Kavout, Zacks AI, Pricefx

Step 3: Automate One Financial Process at a Time

- Start small – Automate one financial task first (e.g., invoicing).
- Monitor results – Track efficiency, accuracy, and cost savings.
- Expand AI integration once it's working well.

Example: A company started by automating invoice tracking. When it worked flawlessly, they expanded AI to budgeting, fraud detection, and payroll.

Step 4: Train Your Team & Monitor AI Performance

- Ensure employees understand AI-powered finance tools and how to use them properly.
- Review AI-generated financial reports regularly to catch any errors or anomalies.
- Stay updated on AI finance trends to take advantage of new tools and features.

Example: A finance team using AI-powered forecasting reduced cash flow surprises by 80% because they knew exactly what to expect in the coming months.

Final Thoughts: AI Makes Money Management Smarter & Easier

- AI-powered finance tools eliminate human errors, improve efficiency, and increase business profitability.
- AI helps businesses automate bookkeeping, budgeting, payroll, and fraud detection—saving time and money.
- The businesses that embrace AI-powered finance strategies will have a competitive edge in the future economy.

In the next chapter, we'll explore AI in leadership—how AI is transforming business decision-making, team management, and company growth.

Ready to use AI to lead smarter and scale faster? Let's go!

Chapter 7
AI and Leadership – How to Build a Future-Proof Business

Introduction: The Future of Leadership is AI-Driven

Leadership has always been about making smart decisions, guiding teams, and driving business growth. But today, the best leaders aren't just relying on intuition or experience—they're using AI-powered insights to lead with precision and confidence.

- AI is changing how leaders make decisions, manage teams, and scale businesses.
- AI helps leaders process complex data, predict trends, and optimize strategies in real time.
- The most successful business owners and CEOs are using AI to gain a competitive edge.

In this chapter, you'll learn how to:

- Use AI to make smarter, faster, and more profitable business decisions
- Leverage AI for better team management, productivity, and leadership efficiency
- Stay ahead of industry trends with AI-powered forecasting and analytics
- Balance AI automation with human leadership to build a thriving company culture

By the end of this chapter, you'll have a clear strategy for integrating AI into your leadership approach—allowing you to lead smarter, scale faster, and future-proof your business.

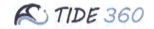

Why AI is the Secret Weapon for Modern Leaders

Leadership today requires more than experience—it requires adaptability.

- AI is revolutionizing leadership by providing real-time data, predictive insights, and automation tools.
- Instead of relying on outdated reports, leaders can make data-driven decisions instantly.
- AI doesn't replace leadership—it enhances it by reducing guesswork and increasing efficiency.

Companies that integrate AI into leadership strategies report:

- Faster decision-making with real-time AI-powered insights
- More effective teams thanks to AI-driven productivity tools
- Higher profitability due to AI-optimized operations and forecasting
- Stronger company culture by balancing automation with human leadership

The most successful leaders aren't fighting AI—they're using it as their most powerful business tool.

The 5 Ways AI is Transforming Leadership

1. AI for Smarter, Data-Driven Decision Making

- **AI-Powered Business Insights** – AI analyzes millions of data points in seconds, providing leaders with clear, actionable insights.
- **Predictive Analytics** – AI forecasts trends, helping leaders make future-proof business decisions.
- **AI for Risk Assessment** – AI identifies potential risks and opportunities before they impact the business.

Example: A CEO using AI-driven market analysis predicted a major shift in customer demand and adjusted their strategy—leading to a 20% revenue increase.

Best AI Decision-Making Tools:

IBM Watson, Tableau AI, ThoughtSpot

2. AI for Team Management & Productivity

- **AI-Powered Task Delegation** – AI suggests which employees should handle specific tasks based on their skills and workload.
- **Automated Meeting Summaries** – AI tools transcribe and summarize meetings, ensuring no important detail is lost.
- **AI for Performance Tracking** – AI analyzes employee productivity and suggests ways to optimize team performance.

Example: A company using AI-powered productivity tracking saw a 35% boost in efficiency because employees were assigned tasks based on real-time workload balancing.

Best AI Team Management Tools:

Asana AI, ClickUp AI, Notion AI, Clockwise

3. AI for Enhancing Workplace Communication

- **AI-Powered Email & Messaging Optimization** – AI helps leaders write more effective emails and team messages.
- **AI for Conflict Resolution** – AI analyzes team communication and detects potential conflicts before they escalate.
- **Real-Time Language Translation** – AI-powered tools break down language barriers, making global teams more connected.

Example: A business with remote international teams used AI-powered translation tools to improve collaboration and cut miscommunication issues by 50%.

Best AI Communication Tools:

Grammarly AI, Otter.ai, DeepL Translator

4. AI for Leadership Development & Training

- **AI-Powered Personalized Learning** – AI creates custom learning paths for leaders and employees based on strengths and weaknesses.
- **Automated Leadership Coaching** – AI-driven coaching tools provide feedback on leadership style and decision-making.
- **AI for Emotional Intelligence (EQ) Analysis** – AI analyzes communication styles and suggests improvements to strengthen leadership skills.

Example: A company that integrated AI-powered leadership coaching into their executive training increased manager effectiveness scores by 40%.

Best AI Leadership Development Tools:

Receptiviti AI, Butterfly.ai, CoachHub

5. AI for Scaling Business Growth & Innovation

- **AI-Powered Market Research** – AI scans industry trends and consumer behavior to uncover new opportunities.
- **AI for Competitive Analysis** – AI compares business performance with competitors, highlighting areas for growth.
- **AI-Driven Innovation Strategies** – AI suggests new business models and revenue streams based on market demand.

Example: A business used AI to analyze global expansion opportunities, leading them to enter a new market that increased revenue by 60%.

Best AI Business Growth Tools:

Crayon AI, AlphaSense, SparkBeyond

How to Integrate AI into Your Leadership Strategy

Step 1: Identify Leadership Areas That Need AI Support

Ask yourself:

- Where do I struggle with decision-making due to lack of data?
- Which leadership tasks take up too much time?
- Where could AI help improve communication and team efficiency?

Example: If you spend hours each week analyzing business reports, AI-powered business intelligence tools can generate instant reports with actionable insights.

Step 2: Choose the Right AI Leadership Tools

- **AI for Decision-Making & Analytics:** IBM Watson, Tableau AI, ThoughtSpot
- **AI for Team Management & Productivity:** Asana AI, ClickUp AI, Clockwise
- **AI for Workplace Communication:** Grammarly AI, Otter.ai, DeepL Translator
- **AI for Leadership Training & Development:** Butterfly.ai, CoachHub, Receptiviti AI
- **AI for Business Growth & Market Research:** AlphaSense, Crayon AI, SparkBeyond

Step 3: Implement AI in One Leadership Area at a Time

- Start small – Choose one leadership task to automate (e.g., meeting summaries).
- Test & measure results – See how AI improves decision-making and efficiency.

- Expand AI integration once you're comfortable with the first implementation.

Example: A CEO started using AI for automated task delegation and saw productivity improvements, then expanded AI into predictive analytics for market trends.

Step 4: Balance AI Automation with Human Leadership

- Don't rely entirely on AI – Use AI as a support tool, but keep human judgment in leadership decisions.
- Train your team on AI usage – Help employees understand how AI enhances rather than replaces leadership.
- Monitor AI effectiveness regularly – Adjust AI strategies based on real-world performance.

Final Thoughts: AI Leadership is the Future – Will You Adapt?

- AI is not replacing leadership—it's enhancing it.
- The best leaders use AI to make smarter decisions, manage teams effectively, and drive business growth.
- AI-powered leadership is the key to future-proofing your business and staying ahead of the competition.

Ready to lead smarter and scale faster? Let's go!

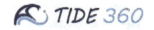

Chapter 8
The Future of AI & Business Innovation – What's Next?

Introduction: AI is Just Getting Started

Artificial Intelligence is not slowing down—it's accelerating. Businesses that think AI is a trend will be left behind, while those who integrate AI into their strategies will lead the future.

- AI is rapidly evolving, introducing new capabilities that will reshape entire industries.
- The businesses that stay ahead of AI advancements will dominate their markets.
- AI-driven companies will be more innovative, efficient, and profitable than ever before.

In this chapter, we'll explore:

- The top AI trends shaping the future of business
- How AI will revolutionize industries beyond automation
- How businesses can stay competitive as AI continues to advance

By the end of this chapter, you'll have a clear vision of what's next for AI and how to position your business for long-term success.

The 5 Biggest AI Trends That Will Shape the Future of Business

1. AI-Generated Creativity & Content

- AI is already writing blogs, designing graphics, and even composing music.
- Future AI will generate fully automated branding, storytelling, and marketing campaigns.
- Businesses will use AI-generated content to create faster, high-quality marketing materials.

Real-World Example: Coca-Cola is using AI-powered ad generation tools to create personalized digital marketing campaigns at scale—saving time and increasing engagement.

AI Creativity Tools to Try:

MidJourney AI, Jasper AI, Synthesia AI

2. AI-Powered Hyper-Personalization

- AI will create fully customized customer experiences in real time.
- Businesses will move from broad marketing campaigns to AI-driven, one-on-one engagement.
- AI will predict what customers want before they even ask—offering solutions instantly.

Real-World Example: Amazon's AI-driven recommendation engine already accounts for 35% of its total sales. Future AI will make shopping even more tailored and predictive.

AI Personalization Tools to Try:

Salesforce Einstein, Adobe Sensei, Dynamic Yield

3. AI-Driven Automation & Autonomous Businesses

- Businesses will rely on AI for decision-making at every level.
- AI-powered automation will handle everything from customer service to logistics.
- Fully autonomous AI-run businesses will emerge, requiring minimal human intervention.

Real-World Example: Tesla is developing AI-powered factories where robots and AI-driven systems manage production, reducing costs and increasing output.

AI Automation Tools to Try:

UiPath, WorkFusion, Zapier AI

4. AI in Finance, Security & Fraud Prevention

- AI will detect fraudulent transactions faster than any human analyst.
- AI-powered security tools will prevent cyberattacks before they happen.
- Businesses will use AI to manage investments, predict stock trends, and automate budgeting.

Real-World Example: PayPal's AI fraud detection system scans transactions in milliseconds, preventing fraudulent activity and saving businesses billions annually.

AI Finance & Security Tools to Try:

Feedzai, Forter, Kavout

5. AI Ethics, Regulations & Responsible Innovation

- AI will raise critical questions about privacy, bias, and responsible usage.
- Governments will introduce stricter AI regulations to prevent misuse.
- Businesses that adopt ethical AI practices early will build trust and credibility.

Real-World Example: Google is investing in AI ethics research to ensure its AI models are transparent, fair, and unbiased. Companies that fail to prioritize AI ethics risk losing customer trust.

AI Ethics & Compliance Tools to Try: OpenAI Moderation, IBM AI Fairness 360, Google AI Explainability

How Businesses Must Prepare for the Future of AI

Step 1: Develop an AI-First Strategy

- AI should not be an afterthought—it must be part of your core business model.
- Invest in AI-powered automation, personalization, and analytics now.
- Create an AI roadmap for the next 5-10 years to stay ahead.

Example: Businesses that invested in e-commerce early dominated the retail space—AI will create the same shift across industries.

Step 2: Train Your Team to Work Alongside AI

- AI won't replace all jobs, but it will change them—prepare your team to adapt.
- Invest in AI literacy and training to help employees maximize AI's potential.
- Encourage a mindset of innovation, experimentation, and AI-powered efficiency.

Example: Companies that trained employees on AI-powered tools saw higher productivity and faster adoption of automation strategies.

Step 3: Balance AI Innovation with Ethical Responsibility

- AI must be used responsibly to avoid bias, privacy violations, and unethical practices.
- Be transparent with customers about how AI is used in your business.
- Follow ethical AI guidelines to maintain trust and credibility.

Example: Businesses that adopt ethical AI policies now will avoid future lawsuits, scandals, and loss of customer trust.

Step 4: Stay Adaptable & Keep Evolving with AI Trends

- AI is constantly evolving—businesses that don't keep up will fall behind.
- Stay updated on the latest AI developments and adjust strategies accordingly.
- Be ready to pivot when new AI opportunities arise.

Example: Just as social media changed marketing forever, AI will reshape how businesses operate—those who adapt will thrive.

Final Thoughts: AI is the Future—Are You Ready?

- AI is not a passing trend—it's the foundation of the next era of business.
- Businesses that embrace AI now will shape the future of innovation.
- The key to success is continuous AI-driven learning, adaptation, and ethical leadership.

In the next chapter, we'll explore how to take action now to integrate AI into your business—without delay.

Ready to future-proof your business and stay ahead of the competition? Let's go!

Chapter 9:
Your AI Business Action Plan – Implement AI the Right Way with TIDE 360

Introduction: AI is the Future—TIDE 360 is the Solution

You've seen how AI is transforming industries, creating new opportunities for efficiency, scalability, and profitability. But here's the reality:

- AI alone isn't enough—you need the right strategy to implement it successfully.
- Many businesses waste time and money on AI tools without a clear roadmap.
- AI must be integrated strategically to maximize its impact—this is where TIDE 360 comes in.

TIDE 360 was designed to eliminate the guesswork and provide businesses with a structured, results-driven approach to AI adoption.

*TIDE stands for **Transformation through Innovation, Development, and Excellence**—our core mission is to help businesses harness AI to drive sustainable success.*

TIDE also represents a proven AI framework:

- **T – Technology**: Implement cutting-edge AI tools that streamline and optimize your business.
- **I – Innovation**: Use AI to revolutionize marketing, sales, and operations.
- **D – Data**: Leverage AI-driven analytics for smarter, faster decision-making.
- **E – Execution**: Ensure seamless AI adoption with expert strategy and hands-on implementation.

At TIDE 360, we don't just introduce AI to your business—we make sure it works for you, delivering measurable growth while eliminating inefficiencies.

Your AI Business Roadmap with TIDE 360

Step 1: Book a Free AI Strategy Session

The first step to AI success is understanding how AI fits into your unique business model.

- We begin with an AI assessment to determine the best automation and optimization opportunities.
- We analyze your operations, customer engagement, and financial processes to pinpoint inefficiencies.
- You receive a tailored AI blueprint detailing how to integrate AI successfully.

How to Get Started: Schedule your free TIDE 360 AI Strategy Session today.

*Call us now or visit **www.TIDE360.ai** to book a consultation.*

Step 2: Choose the Right TIDE 360 AI Solutions for Your Business

AI implementation isn't a one-size-fits-all approach—you need a solution that fits your growth goals.

- **TIDE 360 Webinar (Free)**
  The inside look at their journey to profitable, sustainable AI integration in 2025.
  When they register for the webinar, they will get a choice of a SMILE system eBook as a complimentary gift ($27 Value)

- **Access to TIDE 360 Agents ($297mo.)**
  - o Secretary
  - o Accountant
  - o Training
- **TIDE 360 Group coaching 6 weeks ($997per person)**
  - o Six 60 min online group sessions over a 6-week period to guide stakeholders through a wealthy and healthy innovation process.
- **TIDE 360 by Your side coaching 12 weeks ($9,997)**
  - o (1 on 1) 12x 90–120-minute group online sessions to guide them through the implementation of the TIDE 360 bots into their businesses.
  - o Information sessions
  - o Hot seats and Q&A
- **DFY: TIDE 360 (1 on 1) consulting (Starting $49,997)**
  - o Business Assessments
  - o Business AI-ification and automation consulting
  - o Implementable tailored solution for your organization
- **TIDE 360 Implementation**
  - o Implementation of business consultation solutions
  - o Complete AI-ification of your business as identified in your consultation
  - o Support of the tailored solution for your organization

Which AI package is right for you? Book a consultation and find out.

Call us today to start leveraging AI the right way.

Step 3: Implement AI with TIDE 360's Seamless Execution Model

One of the biggest challenges businesses face when adopting AI is poor execution.

- TIDE 360 removes the complexity and ensures AI is implemented strategically.
- Our team handles AI integration, training, and workflow optimization—so you don't have to.
- We ensure AI tools work seamlessly with your current business processes.

Why struggle with AI alone when TIDE 360 can handle it for you?

Schedule your AI Implementation Call today!

Step 4: Scale & Optimize with AI-Driven Data Insights

AI is not a one-time fix—it's an evolving system that needs continuous refinement.

- TIDE 360 provides ongoing AI performance tracking to ensure your business continues to grow.
- We analyze AI-driven data insights to optimize marketing, sales, and operational strategies.
- We fine-tune AI tools based on real-time results to maximize ROI.

With TIDE 360, AI isn't just installed—it's continuously optimized for long-term success.

Step 5: Future-Proof Your Business with TIDE 360's AI Innovation Lab

AI is evolving fast, and staying ahead of the curve is essential.

- TIDE 360's AI Innovation Lab ensures your business remains at the forefront of AI advancements.
- We introduce new AI capabilities before your competitors even hear about them.
- You gain access to AI-powered forecasting tools that predict industry shifts before they happen.

Want to stay ahead of the AI revolution?

Join TIDE 360's AI Innovation Lab today.

Why Businesses Trust TIDE 360 for AI Integration

- "We knew AI was important, but we didn't know where to start. TIDE 360 took the guesswork out of AI adoption, and now our marketing, sales, and customer service are fully automated and more profitable than ever."
- "TIDE 360 gave us a complete AI strategy—no more wasting time on random tools. Our efficiency has skyrocketed, and we're scaling faster than ever before."
- "AI implementation felt overwhelming until we worked with TIDE 360. Their structured approach made integration seamless, and our revenue has increased by 40%."

Don't take our word for it—see the impact for yourself.

Book a free AI strategy call today!

Final Thoughts: AI is the Future—TIDE 360 is the Solution

- AI is no longer optional—it's the foundation of long-term business success.
- TIDE 360 makes AI adoption simple, strategic, and results-driven.
- You don't have to navigate AI alone—our team will guide you every step of the way.

The future of business is AI-driven, and TIDE 360 is your gateway to success.

Click this [link] or visit [your website] to start your AI journey with TIDE 360 today!

Your AI-powered success story starts here. Let's go!

Introduction to the Journaling Section

Welcome to the Journaling Section of **SMILE and SCALE**! You've just explored powerful strategies, frameworks, and tools to help your business leverage AI for growth and sustainability. Now, it's time to take those insights and transform them into real action.

In this section, you'll find a series of prompts designed to guide you through self-reflection, planning, and goal-setting. Each chapter of the book has been paired with five thought-provoking prompts that will help you dig deeper into the concepts and apply them to your unique business context. These prompts are more than just a chance to jot down ideas—they are an invitation to actively shape the future of your business using the power of AI.

Why is journaling important, especially in a book about business growth and AI?

Journaling is a powerful tool for clarity. By writing down your thoughts, you'll begin to connect the dots between the information you've learned and the reality of your business. It forces you to slow down and think critically about what's working, what needs improvement, and how you can use AI to address specific challenges. When you put pen to paper (or fingers to keyboard), it opens up space for creativity and insight that often gets lost in the hustle of everyday business operations.

Journaling helps with accountability. By setting aside time to reflect on the prompts, you are committing to a process of growth and action. This dedicated space will allow you to create an AI implementation plan that's uniquely yours—something you can refer back to as you move

through each stage of the AI adoption process. It's a record of your evolving business mindset and your journey to scale with AI.

Journaling is about personalizing your learning. Every business is different. While the concepts in **SMILE and SCALE** provide a powerful roadmap, your specific context and challenges are what will make this process truly transformative. These prompts are not one-size-fits-all answers—they are a way for you to adapt the information to your needs, figure out where to start, and decide what steps will drive the most impact for your company.

Journaling unlocks strategic thinking. The reflective nature of journaling encourages you to think beyond your current situation. It helps you visualize the bigger picture: where you want your business to go, how AI can get you there, and what new possibilities are waiting to be explored. The insights you gain from writing down your thoughts will spark creative ideas that can push your business forward in ways you may not have considered.

Finally, journaling helps you stay focused. AI can seem overwhelming at first. There are so many tools, trends, and potential disruptions to consider. But journaling gives you a chance to break it down, reflect on one piece at a time, and keep your vision clear. It brings structure to your AI strategy, guiding you from abstract concepts to tangible next steps that are aligned with your long-term goals.

As you work through the prompts, take your time. There are no right or wrong answers—this is about your journey and the future you want to create. Use these pages as a space to brainstorm, plan, and get excited about the possibilities that lie ahead.

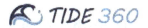

Once you finish each set of prompts, you'll have a clear action plan for applying the SMILE philosophy and the TIDE 360 framework to your business. The journaling exercises will give you the confidence to step forward into the future of AI innovation and lead your business toward sustainable, scalable success.

Let's get started—your AI-powered future is waiting.

Chapter 1:

The AI Revolution – Why Now is the Time to Innovate

Prompt 1:

What are the top 3 areas in your business that could benefit from AI right now? Why?

_____

_____

_____

_____

_____

_____

_____

_____

_____

_____

_____

_____

_____

_____

Prompt 2:

How do you currently feel about integrating AI into your business? What excites you, and what concerns do you?

_____

_____

_____

_____

_____

_____

_____

_____

_____

_____

_____

_____

_____

_____

_____

_____

_____

Prompt 3:

Think of a competitor or a company you admire. How are they using AI, and what can you learn from their approach?

_____

_____

_____

_____

_____

_____

_____

_____

_____

_____

_____

_____

_____

_____

_____

_____

Prompt 4:

Imagine it's one year from today and you've successfully adopted AI into your business. What does your daily workflow look like?

_____

_____

_____

_____

_____

_____

_____

_____

_____

_____

_____

_____

_____

_____

_____

_____

Prompt 5:

What is one decision you've been hesitant to make around innovation or automation? Why have you delayed it—and what would happen if you made that move now?

_____

_____

_____

_____

_____

_____

_____

_____

_____

_____

_____

_____

_____

_____

Chapter 2:
The SMILE Framework for AI-Powered Business Growth

Prompt 1:

Which of the five SMILE pillars—Strategic, Measurable, Inclusive, Long-term, or Ethical—feels most aligned with your current business practices? Which one do you need to focus on more?

_____

_____

_____

_____

_____

_____

_____

_____

_____

_____

_____

_____

Prompt 2:

Think about a recent business decision you made. If you had applied the SMILE framework to that decision, what might you have done differently?

_____

_____

_____

_____

_____

_____

_____

_____

_____

_____

_____

_____

_____

_____

Prompt 3:

Describe how you envision AI contributing to long-term, sustainable growth in your business. What does that look like in practice?

_____

_____

_____

_____

_____

_____

_____

_____

_____

_____

_____

_____

_____

_____

Prompt 4:

What would it mean for your business to become more inclusive through AI? What steps can you take to ensure your systems empower rather than replace?

_____

_____

_____

_____

_____

_____

_____

_____

_____

_____

_____

_____

_____

_____

Prompt 5:

How can you measure the success of AI integration beyond just financial ROI? What metrics matter most to you (e.g., time saved, customer experience, team morale)?

_____

_____

_____

_____

_____

_____

_____

_____

_____

_____

_____

_____

_____

_____

Chapter 3:
AI-Powered Automation – Work Less, Earn More

Prompt 1:

What are 3 repetitive tasks in your daily business operations that you could delegate to AI right now?

_____

_____

_____

_____

_____

_____

_____

_____

_____

_____

_____

_____

_____

_____

Prompt 2:

How would your day-to-day change if you automated 50% of your operational workload? What would you do with the extra time?

_____

_____

_____

_____

_____

_____

_____

_____

_____

_____

_____

_____

_____

_____

_____

_____

_____

Prompt 3:

What fears or resistance do you have around automation? Are they based on facts, emotions, or past experiences?

_____

_____

_____

_____

_____

_____

_____

_____

_____

_____

_____

_____

_____

_____

_____

_____

Prompt 4:

Describe an ideal automated customer journey in your business—from first contact to follow-up. Where could AI improve the experience?

_____

_____

_____

_____

_____

_____

_____

_____

_____

_____

_____

_____

_____

_____

_____

Prompt 5:

What does "working less, earning more" mean to you personally? What would it look like to achieve that balance in the next 6–12 months using AI?

_____

_____

_____

_____

_____

_____

_____

_____

_____

_____

_____

_____

_____

_____

Chapter 4:
The Wealthy & Healthy Approach to AI Strategy

Prompt 1:

In what ways can AI support your *personal* definition of a "wealthy & healthy" business life?

_____

_____

_____

_____

_____

_____

_____

_____

_____

_____

_____

_____

_____

_____

Prompt 2:

Think of a recent investment you made in your business. How could AI have amplified the return on that investment?

_____

_____

_____

_____

_____

_____

_____

_____

_____

_____

_____

_____

_____

_____

_____

Prompt 3:

Where do you currently see imbalance between automation and the human touch in your business? How can you realign?

_____

_____

_____

_____

_____

_____

_____

_____

_____

_____

_____

_____

_____

_____

_____

_____

Prompt 4:

Reflect on a business that inspires you. How do they use AI (or smart systems) to grow ethically and sustainably?

_____

_____

_____

_____

_____

_____

_____

_____

_____

_____

_____

_____

_____

_____

_____

_____

Prompt 5:

What does long-term success look like for you? How can AI play a strategic role in helping you get there *without burnout*?

_____

_____

_____

_____

_____

_____

_____

_____

_____

_____

_____

_____

_____

_____

_____

Chapter 5:
AI-Driven Marketing – Personalization & Profitability at Scale

Prompt 1:

What aspects of your current marketing strategy feel outdated or inefficient? Where could AI help you scale or personalize?

_____

_____

_____

_____

_____

_____

_____

_____

_____

_____

_____

_____

_____

_____

Prompt 2:

Describe your ideal customer journey—from awareness to purchase. How can AI make that journey more seamless and personalized?

_____

_____

_____

_____

_____

_____

_____

_____

_____

_____

_____

_____

_____

_____

_____

Prompt 3:

What kind of data do you already have about your audience? How might
AI help you use it more effectively to drive results?

_____

_____

_____

_____

_____

_____

_____

_____

_____

_____

_____

_____

_____

_____

_____

Prompt 4:

What fears do you have around handing over parts of your marketing to AI? What would help you feel more confident?

_____

_____

_____

_____

_____

_____

_____

_____

_____

_____

_____

_____

_____

_____

_____

_____

Prompt 5:

Imagine your marketing working 24/7 without extra effort from you. What does that look like? What's the first step to making it real?

_____

_____

_____

_____

_____

_____

_____

_____

_____

_____

_____

_____

_____

_____

_____

_____

Chapter 6:
AI-Powered Finance – Smarter Money Management

Prompt 1:

What's one area of your business finances that currently feels disorganized or time-consuming? How could AI simplify it?

_____

_____

_____

_____

_____

_____

_____

_____

_____

_____

_____

_____

_____

_____

George Knowlton

 *TIDE* 360

Prompt 2:

How do you currently track your financial health? Imagine AI giving you real-time insights—what would you want it to tell you?

_____

_____

_____

_____

_____

_____

_____

_____

_____

_____

_____

_____

_____

_____

Prompt 3:

What emotions come up when you think about delegating financial analysis or budgeting to AI? Explore where those feelings come from.

_____

_____

_____

_____

_____

_____

_____

_____

_____

_____

_____

_____

_____

_____

_____

_____

_____

Prompt 4:

Think about a major financial decision you made in the past 12 months. How might AI-powered data have helped you make a more informed choice?

_____

_____

_____

_____

_____

_____

_____

_____

_____

_____

_____

_____

_____

Prompt 5:

What would financial peace of mind look like in your business? What's one AI-driven financial tool or process that could help you move closer to that vision?

_____

_____

_____

_____

_____

_____

_____

_____

_____

_____

_____

_____

_____

_____

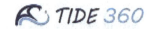
Chapter 7:
AI and Leadership – How to Build a Future-Proof Business

Prompt 1:

How has your leadership style evolved over the past few years? What role could AI play in supporting your growth as a modern leader?

_____

_____

_____

_____

_____

_____

_____

_____

_____

_____

_____

_____

_____

Prompt 2:

What tasks or decisions currently take up too much of your time as a leader? How could AI help you delegate or streamline them?

_____

_____

_____

_____

_____

_____

_____

_____

_____

_____

_____

_____

_____

_____

_____

_____

_____

Prompt 3:

What does being a "future-proof" leader mean to you? Which leadership qualities will be most important in an AI-driven world?

_____

_____

_____

_____

_____

_____

_____

_____

_____

_____

_____

_____

_____

_____

_____

Prompt 4:

Think about your team or collaborators. How could AI empower them to work smarter—not harder—while preserving creativity and motivation?

_____

_____

_____

_____

_____

_____

_____

_____

_____

_____

_____

_____

_____

_____

_____

_____

Prompt 5:

If you could automate one leadership responsibility today, what would it be—and how would that free you to lead more strategically?

_____

_____

_____

_____

_____

_____

_____

_____

_____

_____

_____

_____

_____

_____

Chapter 8:

The Future of AI & Business Innovation – What's Next?

Prompt 1:

What excites you most about the future of AI in business? Describe the ideal AI-enhanced future you envision for your industry.

_____

_____

_____

_____

_____

_____

_____

_____

_____

_____

_____

_____

_____

_____

_____

Prompt 2:

Which of the five AI trends mentioned in this chapter feels most relevant to your business? How can you start preparing for it now?

_____

_____

_____

_____

_____

_____

_____

_____

_____

_____

_____

_____

_____

_____

_____

_____

Prompt 3:

If your business fully embraced AI, what would it look like in 3–5 years? Sketch that vision—what's possible?

_____

_____

_____

_____

_____

_____

_____

_____

_____

_____

_____

_____

_____

_____

_____

George Knowlton

Prompt 4:

What potential challenges or fears do you have about the future of AI?
What can you do today to turn those fears into opportunities?

_____

_____

_____

_____

_____

_____

_____

_____

_____

_____

_____

_____

_____

_____

Prompt 5:

What's one bold innovation you'd love to pursue if time, money, and technology weren't obstacles? Could AI be the bridge to that dream?

_____

_____

_____

_____

_____

_____

_____

_____

_____

_____

_____

_____

_____

_____

_____

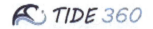

Chapter 9:

Your AI Business Action Plan – Implement AI the Right Way with TIDE 360

Prompt 1:

Based on everything you've learned, what's the first step you will take to begin integrating AI into your business? Why start there?

_____

_____

_____

_____

_____

_____

_____

_____

_____

_____

_____

_____

_____

Prompt 2:

Which area of your business (Marketing, Operations, Finance, etc.) is most in need of AI-driven transformation—and why?

_____

_____

_____

_____

_____

_____

_____

_____

_____

_____

_____

_____

_____

_____

_____

_____

Prompt 3:

Reflect on the TIDE 360 framework. Which of the four pillars (Technology, Innovation, Data, Execution) do you feel most prepared for? Which one needs the most attention?

_____

_____

_____

_____

_____

_____

_____

_____

_____

_____

_____

_____

_____

_____

Prompt 4:

Imagine your business six months after implementing TIDE 360. What has improved? What feedback are you getting from customers and your team?

_____

_____

_____

_____

_____

_____

_____

_____

_____

_____

_____

_____

_____

_____

_____

_____

Prompt 5:

What commitment will you make right now to become an AI-forward leader? How will you hold yourself accountable to that commitment?

_____

_____

_____

_____

_____

_____

_____

_____

_____

_____

_____

_____

_____

_____

www.ingramcontent.com/pod-product-compliance
Lightning Source LLC
LaVergne TN
LVHW051641050326
832903LV00022B/845